Copyright © 2023 by Christen McKey. All rights reserved.

No part of this publication may be reproduced, stored in a retrieval system, or transmitted in any form or by any means, electronic, mechanical, photocopying, recording, or otherwise, without written permission of the publisher.

ISBN 979-8-218-13087-9

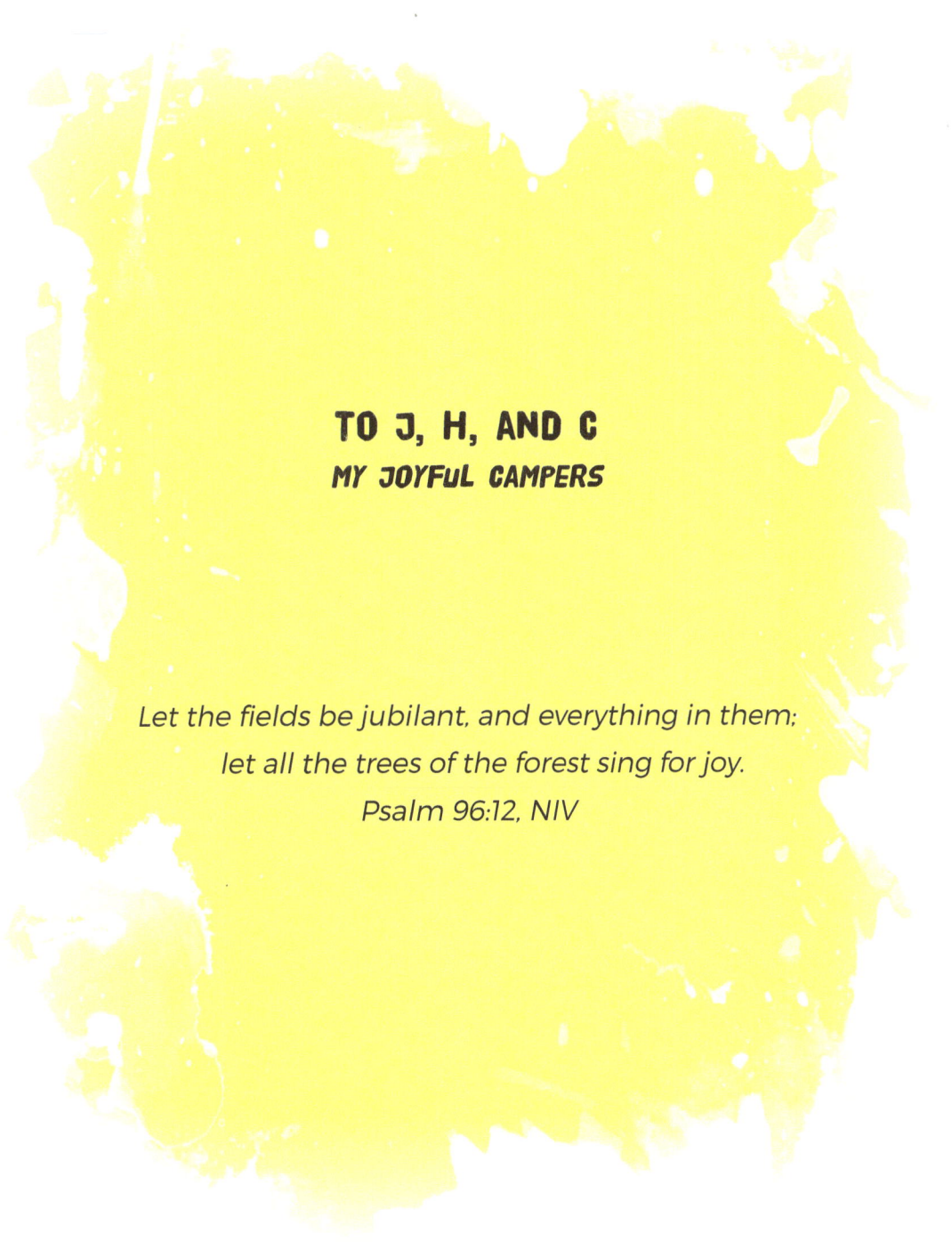

TO J, H, AND C
MY JOYFUL CAMPERS

Let the fields be jubilant, and everything in them;
let all the trees of the forest sing for joy.
Psalm 96:12, NIV

In all seasons of life and all seasons of the year,
POSSIBILITIES ARE ENDLESS. Travel far or stay near.

In eighty degrees or twenty,
In weather, **BOTH GOOD AND BAD.**
For the young and the old, explorers, and soldiers,
For the mom and the dad…

With babies, toddlers, kids, and dogs.
With raccoons, armadillos, bears, and frogs.

With grandparents, with cousins,
With friends, both old and new.
In a **TENT**, **YURT**, **CABIN**, or **CAMPER**, to name a few.

Where else can you find
A classroom so **VAST?**
Learn lessons so fun
And make memories that last?

Worship the Creator in a sanctuary
Only He could make?
REFLECT on his goodness
Where mountains **REFLECT** in a lake?

Sure, there will be **TENSION**
While setting up camp.
PATIENCE will be stretched
As your back gets a cramp.

Work with frozen fingers
Or work up a sweat.
Apologies will be offered
For saying things you regret.

You'll take home
Ember-singed clothes,
Skinned knees,
And stubborn ticks.
You'll have to limit the amount
Of **SOUVENIR ROCKS AND STICKS.**

The smell of campfire smoke will linger for days,
But you'll long for it when the fragrance finally fades.

The **MOUNTAINS** of laundry will resemble
The lovely view from your hike.
And by the ninth load, it'll be enough
To make blood pressure spike.

BUT IT'S ALL WORTH IT,
You know,
All the things you must do
To get ready to go.

It's a lot of work
To plan, pack up,
Unload, and prepare.
But you wouldn't trade
Anything for the
TOGETHERNESS you share.

Not only will time outdoors
Make your heart **HAPPY,**
New tasks and challenges
Will make you quite **SCRAPPY.**

You'll be amazed how
You won't need electronics or toys,
And how the forest sounds at night
Is an incredible noise.

How building a **FORT** will **TRANSPORT**
You back to the olden days,
And how being **CREATIVE** can **CREATE**
Lots of **PARENTAL PRAISE.**

You'll think about the Israelites
Who traveled by tent.
You'll think about simpler days
And how your time is spent.

You'll ponder the power of **FIRE**
And all it can provide;
Light, warmth, and good food
With conversation by its side.

You'll also think of hard times
As flames lick at that pine.
Like fire, God can use trials
To **PURIFY**, **STRENGTHEN**, and **REFINE**.

You can learn how to bait a hook, read a map,
And find **CONSTELLATIONS** in the sky,
The meaning of **PEN PAL**, and how to stay in touch
When it's time to say goodbye.

You'll be surprised at how much fun you can have
In a **CREEK** with a pail,
And how your tired legs can take you farther
Up that **MOUNTAIN TRAIL.**

That water can taste better than **ANY** drink,
When you're so hot from that hike
That you're starting to stink.

You'll have questions, like
"HOW CAN A SLEEPING BAG KEEP YOU SO WARM?"

And "HOW DOES A TENT RAINFLY WORK IN A STORM?"

"WHY DOES SMOKE BURN YOUR EYES?"
"SO THAT'S A SUNRISE?"

"WHY IS MOM SWEEPING THE DIRT?"
"WILL THIS SPIKEY LEAF HURT?"

"IS THIS PATH A TRAIL?"
"IS THIS MOTH A MALE?"

"WHY'S THE SMOKE AIMING FOR ME?"
"IS A YURT LIKE A TEEPEE?"

"HOW IS IT SO DARK?"
"WHO OWNS THIS PARK?"

"WILL I GET TO SEE A BEAR?"
"WHY'S THERE A HOLE IN MY CHAIR?"

"CAN RACCOONS UNZIP ZIPPERS?"
"ARE THOSE STARS THE DIPPERS?"

"IS THAT BIG TREE AN OAK?"
"WHY DOES FIRE MAKE SMOKE?"

You'll learn to be grateful
For even the small things,
And build strength and courage
For all that life brings.

You'll develop character with
Each difficult situation.
The **FRUITS OF THE SPIRIT** are
Ripe for picking on this vacation.

You'll appreciate the fresh, cool air
Without the **CONDITIONING**,
And the heat of the fire with the
Right **CAMP CHAIR POSITIONING**.

You'll have fun researching each and every insect,
And surprising Mom with animal bones to inspect.

You'll discover the
"EVERYTHING TASTES BETTER WHEN CAMPING" mystery,
And all camping food is considered healthy and junk-free.

How reading a **BOOK** outside is better than reading indoors,
And campsite duties are more fun than household chores.

You can learn basic skills
Of survival, problem-solving,
And first aid,
And how to hang a **HAMMOCK**
In the perfect spot in the shade.

How to start a fire with
The help of Dad and some flint,
And give **PURPOSE** to all that
Useless, fluffy dryer lint.

When it comes time to venture out onto the lake,
Be sure to sit still in that kayak, **FOR GOODNESS' SAKE**.

Unless you are hot and ready to take a dip,
Then, **BY ALL MEANS**, go right ahead and make her flip.

You'll meet camp hosts, park hosts,
And rangers,
Who keep the park clean, teach skills,
And warn of dangers.

Someday YOU may even pursue a park career,
Or think how great it would be to volunteer.

You'll find that rules while camping
Differ from those at home.
DIRTY hands at the table
And **WIDER BOUNDARIES** to roam.

Holes in your clothes?
NO SWEAT.

Skip a shower?
YOU BET.

Stay up later?
FINE WITH ME.

Need to pee?
JUST PICK A TREE.

Brush your hair?
I DON'T CARE.

Forget the flossing?
THAT SEEMS FAIR.

Another s'more?
YES, YOU MAY.

Keep this bug?
WELL, JUST FOR THE DAY.

Whether you stay at a campground with **AMENITIES** galore,
Or choose **PRIMITIVE CAMPING** with remote areas to explore,

Or pitch a tent in the backyard for the night,
Or go somewhere that requires a plane flight,

Or set up at the beach or the edge of a lake,
Your decision to camp **WON'T BE A MISTAKE.**

You'll meet unique people from all around,
But it'll be **EASY** to find some common ground.

You'll learn more about the **HEARTS** of those that are with you,
Making memories, bonds, and an inside joke or two.

You'll listen to funny stories
Of when the older were younger,
With no idea that one day,
For **THESE TIMES**, you'll hunger.

When you're sharing **THESE MOMENTS**
With those you love,
Sitting around a fire under those **SAME**
Stars you see above,

You'll be thankful for **THESE ADVENTURES**,
So memorable and fun.
They really are **SOME OF THE BEST**
When all is said and done.

So, pause and take a moment to look around.
From the details of the clouds to the ants on the ground,

You can see God's hand in all you explore outside.
Let **HIM** show you; He's the **ULTIMATE GUIDE.**

You'll be a **HAPPY CAMPER**, yes, but so much more.
A **JOYFUL CAMPER**, filled with that **PEACE** you searched for.

Camping is like no other experience you'll find.
It's good for the soul, body, heart, and mind.

Whether you have **MUCH** or whether you have **LITTLE**,
You can **GO ALL OUT** or keep it **SIMPLE AND NON-COMMITTAL**.

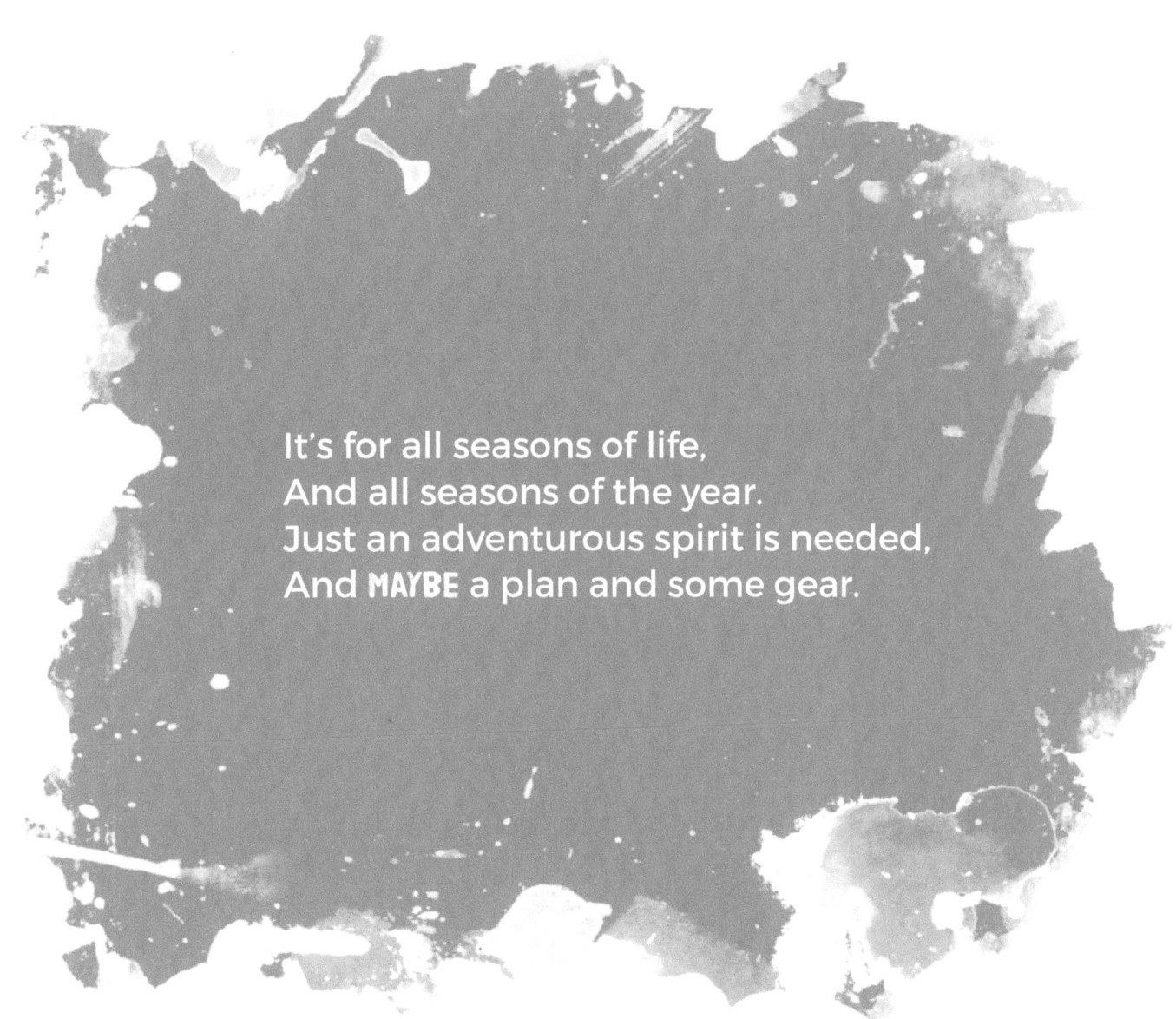

It's for all seasons of life,
And all seasons of the year.
Just an adventurous spirit is needed,
And MAYBE a plan and some gear.

The JOYFUL Glossary

AMENITIES (noun)
Nice features of a campground that make it more desirable and pleasant, like pools, playgrounds, tennis courts, and bathrooms with hot showers.

CABIN (noun)
A wooden house. Usually rustic and located in a place far from traffic and crowds. May contain a bathroom and kitchen. But for the best experience, should not provide a TV or Internet.

CAMPER (noun)
A portable dwelling on wheels that is either pulled by a vehicle, driven, or placed in the bed of a pick-up truck. They come in many shapes and sizes, but backing into a campsite with a camper requires the skills of a ninja.

CONSTELLATION (noun)
A group of stars making a recognizable pattern, like the Big Dipper, the Little Dipper, and Orion. These can more easily be seen when away from city lights, making campgrounds a perfect place for stargazing.

FRUIT OF THE SPIRIT (noun)
"But the fruit of the Spirit is love, joy, peace, patience, kindness, goodness, faithfulness, gentleness, self-control; against such things there is no law." Galatians 5:22-23, ESV

NON-COMMITTAL (adjective)
Not showing a definite decision or opinion of something. Unsure if camping is for you, but wanting to try it. Wisely borrowing equipment instead of buying it. Tagging along with friends on their camping trips. Having an adventurous spirit, but maybe not the time or funds to jump into the world of camping quite yet. A great way to test it out. Because you might just be a joyful camper.

PARENTAL PRAISE (noun)
The smiles, hugs, high-fives, applause, oohs and aahs that you might receive from your parents, grandparents, or other adults in your life when you do something creative, kind, or adventurous.

PATIENCE (noun)
The ability to do hard or uncomfortable things without complaining. The ability to remember all the wonderful blessings of camping while doing the not-so-fun duties of camping.

PEN PAL (noun)
A friend that you write letters to and receive letters from. Letters made from paper and pen or pencil, that arrive in and depart from a mailbox, and travel with the help of a post office and mail carrier. Not the same as an email, video call, text message, or chatsnap thingamajig.

PRIMITIVE CAMPING (noun)
Camping in areas without amenities of any kind. And without electricity, water, or sometimes even cellphone service. Includes peaceful privacy, untouched wilderness, and bragging rights.

REFINE (verb)
The process of improving something by removing unwanted stuff. Fire is often used in this process when refining metals, like gold, and even things like sugar. When you go through something hard, you can learn and grow from that experience. God can remove unwanted stuff from your heart (like selfishness or fear) and you can become a stronger and more beautiful person (like gold), and maybe even a little sweeter too (like sugar).

REFLECT (verb)
To think about something, usually in a deep and quiet way. But also refers to when a surface throws something back that was thrown towards it, like the images of the mountains surrounding a lake can be seen on the smooth surface of the water. Or like when your messy sleeping bag hair is reflected in the bath house mirror after a deep sleep.

SCRAPPY (adjective)
Fiesty and determined. Solving problems and overcoming challenges of a new environment in a fun and creative way.

TENSION (noun)
A certain type of stress that sometimes occurs when multiple people are trying to set up a campsite in a hurry, usually after a long drive and right before the sunlight disappears. Often goes away very quickly with the help of the peaceful outdoors, the love of family members. and several s'mores.

TOGETHERNESS (noun)
Being close to other people. Like when a family of any size is in a tent. Or like when a family talks to each other and does activities with each other. Usually results in a special bond that holds family members and friends together. Like marshmallow goo holds a s'more together, but less messy.

TENT (noun)
A portable shelter made of some type of cloth and supported with poles. Usually requires two or more people to set up, or one person with a large amount of patience and the skills of a ninja.

TRANSPORT (verb)
To move from one place to another. Can happen in real life, like when you travel from your home to an awesome state park in your camper. Or in your imagination, like when the fort you build in the woods becomes the home of a gold miner in the 1800s.

VAST (adjective)
Of very great quantity. A wide space that seems to go on forever. Like when you look around outdoors and you see only nature and hear only nature for as far as the eye can see and the ear can hear. Can take your breath away.

YURT (noun)
A circular tent made of cloth and flexible poles. Orginially used by nomads in Central Asia, but now also offered as a unique camping option in many campgrounds. Like a teepee, but different.

www.ingramcontent.com/pod-product-compliance
Lightning Source LLC
LaVergne TN
LVHW072054070426
835508LV00002B/93